MARIE-NOËLLE HORVATH

Little Felted Animals

CREATE 16 IRRESISTIBLE CREATURES WITH SIMPLE

NEEDLE-FELTING TECHNIQUES

PHOTOGRAPHY BY RICHARD BOUTIN

Watson-Guptill Publications / New York

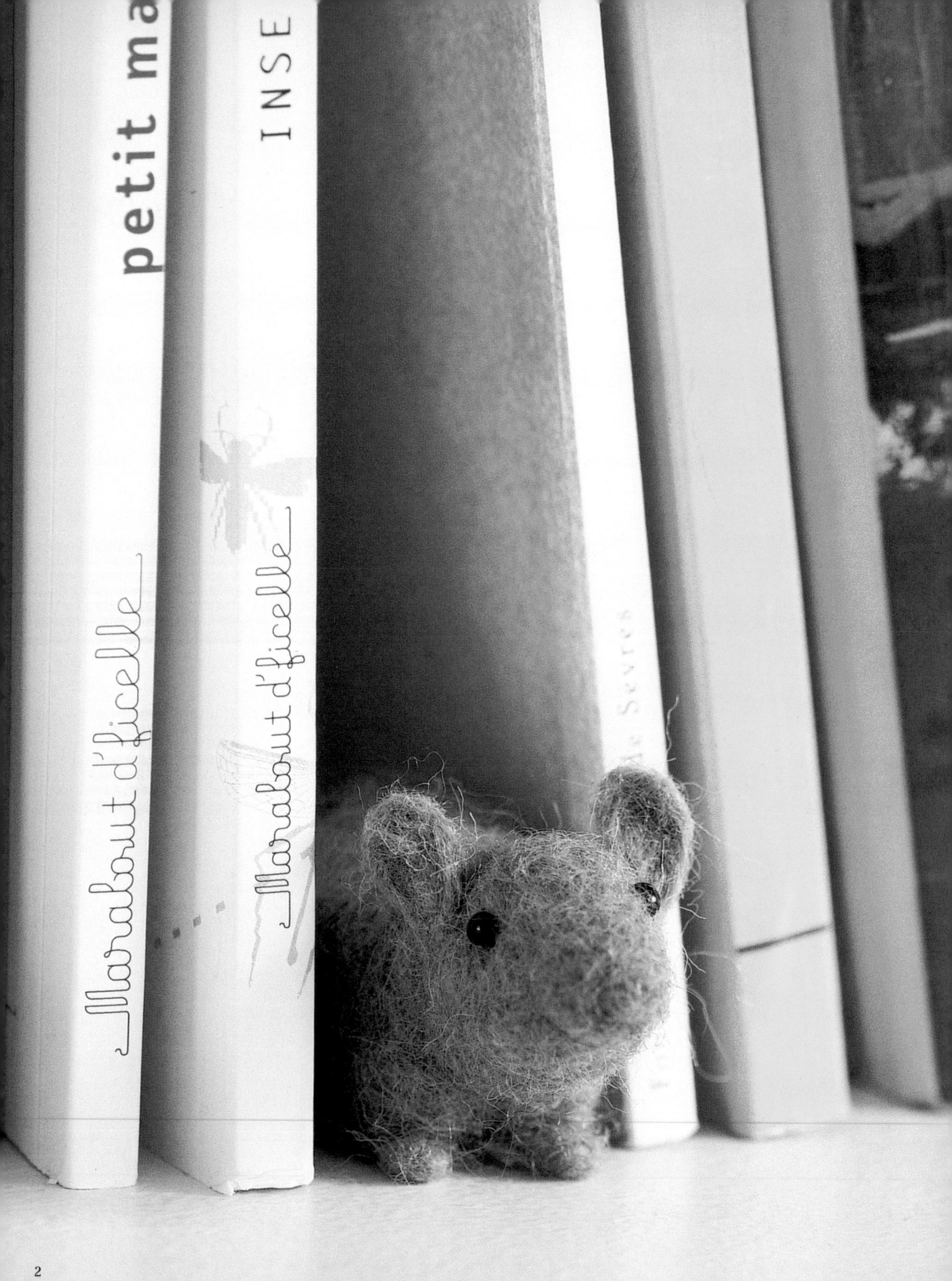
petit ma
INSE
Marabout d'ficelle
Marabout d'ficelle

Contents

Supplies and tips

MATERIALS

Needles
The special barbed felting needles come in several sizes. Use the finest ones for felting the different parts of the body and the coarsest ones for fixing them together. Always insert the needles vertically or they may break. The needles with a wooden handle are more comfortable to use; we've shown two variations of such handles on page 5, but you can use any needle you find comfortable.

Foam felting pad
This serves as a support for the needle felting process. Try not to jab the needle repeatedly into the same place, as this could damage the pad.

Cotton piping cord
This is embedded inside the wool to reinforce the arms and legs of some of the animals. Choose a fairly thin cord. See instructions for using piping cord on page 6.

The eyes
We used glass teddy bears' eyes, which come in different colors and sizes to suit the individual animals. See instructions for sewing on the eyes on page 6.

Sewing needles and thread
A thick sewing needle is needed for making the holes for the eyes. Use a finer needle to sew them in place with thread to match color of the project.

Warning
Be very careful not to stick the needles into your fingers; they are very sharp!

INSTRUCTIONS

The basic process
Needle felting is a process originally developed for making industrial felt. Barbed steel needles are moved in and out of loose woollen fiber to create a matted felt fabric. To create the basic elements, place your piece of woollen fiber on a foam pad and move the felting needle in and out of the fiber in a straight motion until it holds together well and feels spongy when pressed with your finger. Start by making fairly deep jabs to ensure you are felting the inner fibers. Both the angle and the depth of the jab are important for shaping. Jabbing the needle at an angle will cause the fibers to go sideways, and shallow jabbing will felt just the surface fibers. If jabbing at an angle, make sure you keep the needle straight, as it can easily break or be damaged. Turn the fiber shape frequently so that it does not stick to the foam pad. Leave the ends that will be attached to other parts of the body fairly loose.

Shaping the animals
You can achieve the right shapes and bulk by adding more wool, following the designs and the photographs, and by jabbing your needle into the wool at specific points, either deeply or more shallowly. For example, you can flatten the head or define the mouth in this manner.

Making different sizes
The project diagrams are printed at actual size, but you can make each animal smaller or larger as long as you keep the same head-to-body proportion.

Checking the measurements
You can check the measurements of the basic elements and the pieces to be modeled by superimposing them on the diagrams.

SEWING
NEEDLES

FELTING
NEEDLES

SEWING THREAD

EYES

FOAM FELTING PAD

FOAM FELTING PAD

COTTON PIPING
CORD

SCISSORS

FELTING NEEDLES
MOUNTED IN WOODEN
HANDLES

Wool and eyes

COMBED WOOL AND CARDED WOOL

There are two types of wool: combed wool and carded wool.

Combed wool fibers are longer and have been cleansed by the combing process.

Carded wool fibers are more tangled and often contain impurities (scraps of straw, seeds, etc.), which must be removed before felting.

You can use either type of wool; choose according to the desired color of your projects.

HOW TO USE THE PIPING CORD

For some animals, the legs or the arms need to be reinforced by a length of cotton piping cord:
- Cut a length of piping cord slightly shorter than the total length of the leg.
- Take a little wool and jab lightly with the felting needle to create a flat surface.
- Place the length of cord in the center.
- Roll the wool around the cord and needle it some more, then shape the leg.
- Roll it between your palms and then needle it again.
- To form the foot, mark the ankle fold with the needle by jabbing it into the base of the leg.
- Leave an end of unworked wool at the top of the leg with which to attach it to the body.
- Make the other legs in the same way.
- Attach the legs by felting the end of unworked wool onto the body, jabbing with the felting needle to fix them in place.

SEWING ON THE EYES

To attach the eyes, follow the diagram and the following steps:
- Use a thick sewing needle to make holes in the felt for the eyes.
- Push the thinner threaded sewing needle into the hole, then place the eye in the hole, making sure the eye shaft is firmly embedded.
- Push the needle through the back of the head.
- Tie off the thread with a firm knot.

THE ANIMAL SHAPES IN THIS BOOK

There are three basic body shapes used in the projects: birds, short-legged animals, and long-legged animals. On the following pages, you will find step-by-step instructions and photographs illustrating the basic methods for creating these standard shapes, including guidance on how to make your animal shapes sit up and when to use piping cord in the limbs.

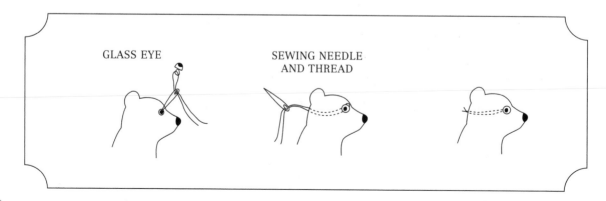

GLASS EYE   SEWING NEEDLE AND THREAD

Color palette

MOTTLED GRAY

WHITE

PINK

BEIGE

MOTTLED GRAY

ORANGE

GRAY

MOTTLED LIGHT BROWN

RUST RED

BLACK

BROWN

DARK RED

STEP-BY-STEP PROCESS

THE BODY

Take a strip of black wool and roll it into a tube. Then jab through with the felting needle to seal it. Leave an end of unworked wool at the top for attaching the head.

THE HEAD

Take a strip of black wool and shape it into a dense ball with the felting needle. Join the head to the body by placing the unworked wool left at the top of the body onto the head.

THE TAIL

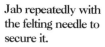

Jab repeatedly with the felting needle to secure it.

Form the tail out of black wool, jabbing it repeatedly to give it the required shape and leaving an unworked end to attach to the body. Fix the tail in place by needling the end onto the body.

THE LEGS

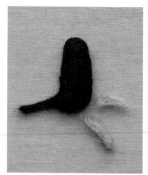   

Take some mottled light brown wool and form the legs, needling them into the required V shape. Roll them between the palms, leaving the wool at the bottom of the V shape unworked. Attach the legs by needling these ends onto the body.

THE BEAK

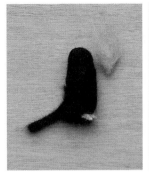

Form the beak from orange wool, leaving the wider end unworked for attaching to the head.
Use the felting needle to fix it in place.

THE WINGS

Form two wings from black wool, leaving unworked ends for attaching them to the body.
Fix them at the wing base only, by needling the ends onto the body.

THE GENERAL SHAPE

Add more black wool, especially around the beak, to give the
head an attractive shape. To achieve a good balance between
outline and bulk, check your work against the diagrams.

THE EYES

Make holes with a sewing needle for
the eyes. The shaft of the eyes should be
firmly embedded in the wool (see page 6).

STEP-BY-STEP PROCESS

THE BODY

 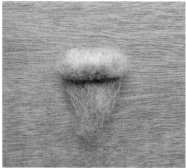 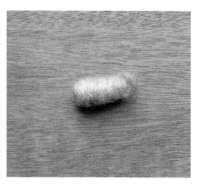

Take a large strip of mottled gray wool and roll it up into a sausage shape. Jab it lightly with the felting needle to secure it. Leave an end of unworked wool at the top for attaching the head.

THE HEAD

 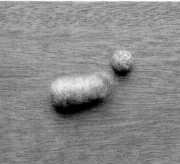 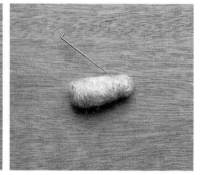

Using the mottled gray wool, form a dense and compact ball with the aid of the felting needle.

Join the two shapes together by needling the unworked body end onto the head.

THE LEGS

  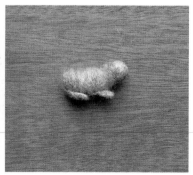

Form the legs with the same gray wool. They should be compact and have an end of unworked wool for attaching to the body.

Attach the legs flat against the torso by needling the unworked ends onto the body.

Shaping a short-legged animal

THE EARS

Using a little mottled gray wool, form the ears, leaving an end of unworked wool for attaching to the head. Add a smaller amount of pink wool to the inner side of each ear.

Attach the ears by needling the ends onto the head.

THE TAIL   ## THE NOSE

With a little of the mottled gray wool, form a fairly soft ball. Leave an end for attaching to the body. Fix it in place by needling the end onto the rear of the body.

Add a very thin strip of black wool to form the nose.

THE GENERAL SHAPE   ## THE EYES

Add more mottled gray wool around the nose, thighs, and neck. Jab with the felting needle to define the muscles.

Make holes with a sewing needle for the eyes. The shaft of the eyes should be firmly embedded in the wool (see page 6).

STEP-BY-STEP PROCESS

THE BODY

 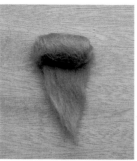

THE HEAD

 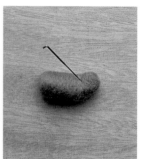

Take a large strip of dark gray wool and roll it into a sausage shape. Jab lightly with the felting needle to secure it. Leave an end of unworked wool at the top for attaching the head.

Make a ball from dark gray wool and join the two parts by needling the loose end of the body onto the head.

THE LEGS

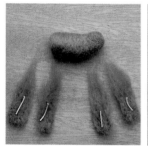 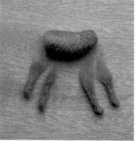 

Cut four lengths of piping cord. Take some strips of the wool and flatten the surface by jabbing with the felting needle. Place a piece of cord in the center of each strip and roll the wool around it. Jab it with the felting needle and then roll it again, leaving a loose end at the top of each strip.

Mark the angle of the foot by jabbing the felting needle into the base of the leg. Attach the legs by needling their ends onto the body.

THE EARS

  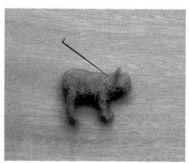

Take a little dark gray wool and form the ears, leaving ends for attaching to the head. Add a little pink wool into the inner side of each ear.

Attach the ears by needling the ends to the head.

THE TAIL

Roll a thin strip of gray wool between your palms. Shape the tail with the felting needle and then roll again between the palms until it is quite compact, leaving an unworked end. Fix in place by needling the end onto the body.

THE GENERAL SHAPE   THE NOSE

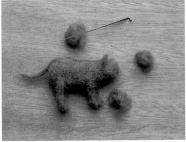  

Add more gray wool around the mouth, the top of the legs, and the chest and neck. Define the muscles by jabbing with the felting needle. To achieve the best balance between outline and bulk, check your work against the diagrams.

Affix a little ball of black wool to the end of the muzzle for the nose.

THE EYES   THE MOUTH

Make holes with a sewing needle for the eyes. The shaft of the eyes should be firmly embedded in the wool (see page 6).

Attach fine strips of black wool for the mouth and then define the lips using the felting needle.

A Family of Penguins EMPERORS OF THE SNOW

ON AN ICY PERCH *Polar Bear*

3

Baby Seal AMONG THE ICE FLOES

SONGSTER OF THE SKY *Blackbird*

Colors of wool
BLACK, WHITE, ORANGE
Eyes
BROWN, ⅕ inch (5 mm)

18

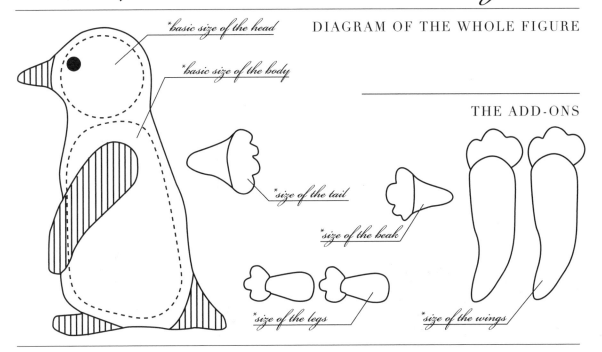

basic size of the head

basic size of the body

DIAGRAM OF THE WHOLE FIGURE

THE ADD-ONS

size of the tail

size of the beak

size of the legs

size of the wings

SHAPING THE BODY

1 Form the basic shapes of the head and body from white wool, leaving an end of unworked wool on the body. Join the two parts by felting the end onto the head with the felting needle.

2 Form the tail in black wool, jabbing with the felting needle to give it the desired shape. Leave an end for attaching to the body. Fix in place by needling the end onto the body.

3 Form the beak from black wool, leaving the base unworked. Fix the beak into place by needling the unworked part onto the head.

4 Form the legs in black wool, giving them the desired shape with the felting needle. Leave an end on each and attach them by needling the ends to the body.

5 Form two wings out of black wool, giving them the desired shape with the felting needle. Leave an end at the top of each for attaching to the body and fix them in place at that end only.

Finishing touches

Improve the shape of the head, beak, neck, chest, and tail by adding more wool, checking against the diagram for guidance.

*

Using black wool, add a thin layer of wool from the top of the head down the back, ending at the tail.

*

Add a touch of orange wool around the top of the chest and a thin strip of the same color along either side of the beak.

*

Sew on the eyes (see diagrams on page 6).

*

Suggestions

Make a family of penguins in different sizes.

Colors of wool
BLACK, GRAY, WHITE
Eyes
BLACK, ⅛ inch (3 mm)

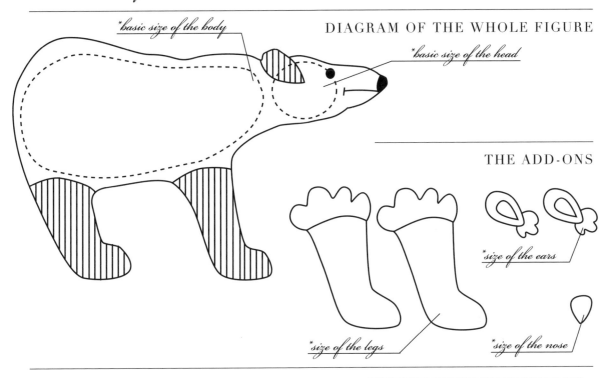

basic size of the body

DIAGRAM OF THE WHOLE FIGURE

basic size of the head

THE ADD-ONS

size of the ears

size of the legs

size of the nose

SHAPING THE BODY

1 Using white wool, make the basic shapes of the head and body, leaving an end of unworked wool on the body. Fix them together by felting this unworked end onto the head with the felting needle.

2 Form the legs with white wool and strips of piping cord (see page 6). Leave an end at the top of each for attaching to the body. Define the toes with some thin vertical strips of gray wool. Fix the legs in place by needling the ends onto the body.

3 For the ears, take some white wool and needle it into the required shapes, leaving ends for attaching to the head. Add a small touch of gray wool to the inner part of each ear and fix ears in place by needling the unworked ends onto the head.

Finishing touches

Add more wool to improve the body proportions, checking against the diagram for accuracy. Needle some extra wool onto the chest to give it a rounded appearance and onto the front of the head to form a muzzle. Add more wool around the neck to cover the joint between the head and the body.

*

Give more bulk to the legs by adding more wool. Define the muscles with the felting needle.

*

Needle a layer of gray wool around the muzzle and add a fine strip to each side to represent the mouth.

*

Make a small ball of black wool for the nose and use the felting needle to attach it to the muzzle.

*

Sew on the eyes
(see diagrams on page 6).

3 *Baby Seal*

DIAGRAM OF THE WHOLE FIGURE

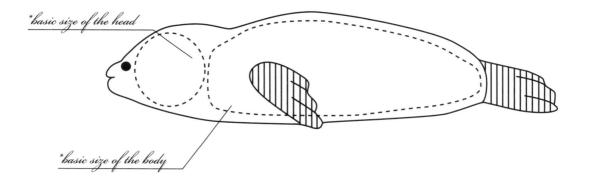

*basic size of the head

*basic size of the body

THE ADD-ONS

*size of the tail (make 2)

*size of the flippers

*size of the nose

SHAPING THE BODY

1 Using white wool, form the basic head and body. Leave an end of unworked wool at the top of the body and join the head and body together by felting this end onto the head with the felting needle.

2 Form the two halves of the tail in white wool, using the felting needle to shape them. Leave ends for attaching them to the body. Fix them in place by needling onto each side of the end of the body.

3 Form the flippers with white wool, needling them into the required shape and leaving ends for attaching to the body. Fix one to each side of the body with the felting needle.

Finishing touches

Improve the proportions of the body by adding more wool, checking against the diagram for accuracy. Add more wool to the front of the head to form the muzzle and around the neck so there is no visible joint between the head and the body.

*

Add a fine strip of black wool for the nose and two little spots on the cheeks, fixing them to the muzzle with the felting needle.

*

Sew on the eyes
(see diagrams on page 6).

Colors of wool
WHITE, BLACK
Eyes
BLACK, ⅛ inch (3 mm)

4 *Blackbird*

DIAGRAM OF THE WHOLE FIGURE

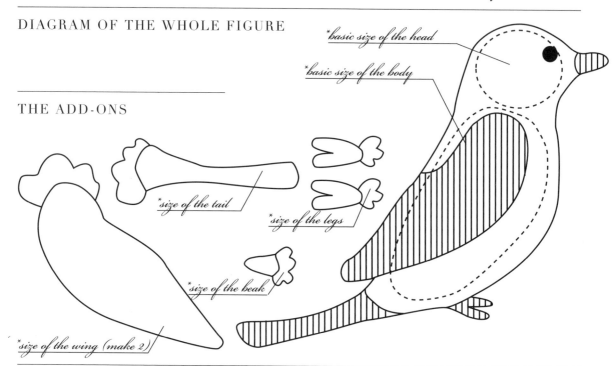

*basic size of the head

*basic size of the body

THE ADD-ONS

*size of the tail

*size of the legs

*size of the beak

*size of the wing (make 2)

SHAPING THE BODY

1 Using black wool, form the basic head and body. Leave an end of unworked wool at the top of the body and join the two pieces together by felting the end onto the head with the felting needle.

2 Form the tail in black wool, needling it into the required shape. Leave an end for attaching to the body with the felting needle.

3 Form the beak from orange wool, leaving the wide end unworked for attaching to the head. Fix it in place with the felting needle.

4 Form the legs from mottled light brown wool, needling them into the required shape and rolling them between your palms. Leave an end at the top of each and attach them to the body with the felting needle.

5 Form the two wings with black wool, using the felting needle to shape them. Leave an unworked end at the top of each and attach them to the body by that end only.

Finishing touches

Improve the proportions of the body by adding more wool, checking against the diagram for accuracy. Needle sufficient extra black wool onto the chest to give it a rounded appearance and add more around the beak and neck to cover the joint between the head and the body.

*

Sew on the eyes
(see diagrams on page 6).

Bunny MEADOW HOPPER

SHORT-HAIR BREED FROM FRANCE *Chartreux Cat*

Welsh Corgi FAVORITE ROYAL DOG

LITTLE AUSTRALIAN TREE CLIMBER *Koala Bear*

Colors of wool
MOTTLED GRAY, PINK, BLACK
Eyes
BROWN, ⅕ inch (5 mm)

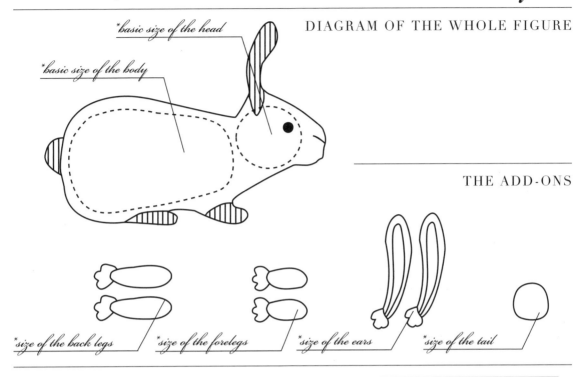

DIAGRAM OF THE WHOLE FIGURE

*basic size of the head

*basic size of the body

THE ADD-ONS

*size of the back legs   *size of the forelegs   *size of the ears   *size of the tail

SHAPING THE BODY

1   Using mottled gray wool, form the basic head and body shapes. Leave an end of unworked wool at the top of the body and join the head and body shapes together by felting this unworked end onto the head with the felting needle.

2   Form the legs in mottled gray wool, needling them into the required shapes and leaving an unworked end on each for attaching them to the body. Fix them in place by needling these ends onto the body.

3   Form the ears from mottled gray wool, needling them into the required shape and leaving an unworked end for attaching them. Add a touch of pink wool to the inside of each ear, and fix them in place by needling the ends onto the head.

4   Using mottled gray wool, form the tail into a small ball, giving it the required shape with the felting needle. Leave an unworked end for attaching it. Fix it in place by needling the end onto the body.

Finishing touches

Improve the proportions of the body by adding more wool, checking against the diagram for accuracy. Needle sufficient extra wool onto the chest to give it a rounded appearance and onto the front of the head to form the muzzle. Add more around the neck to cover the joint between the head and the neck.

*

Add wool to the legs to enlarge them to the correct size and define the muscles with the felting needle.

*

Needle a fine strip of black wool around the edge of the muzzle for the nose.

*

Sew on the eyes
(see diagrams on page 6).

Suggestion

Make another, larger rabbit with longer forelegs.

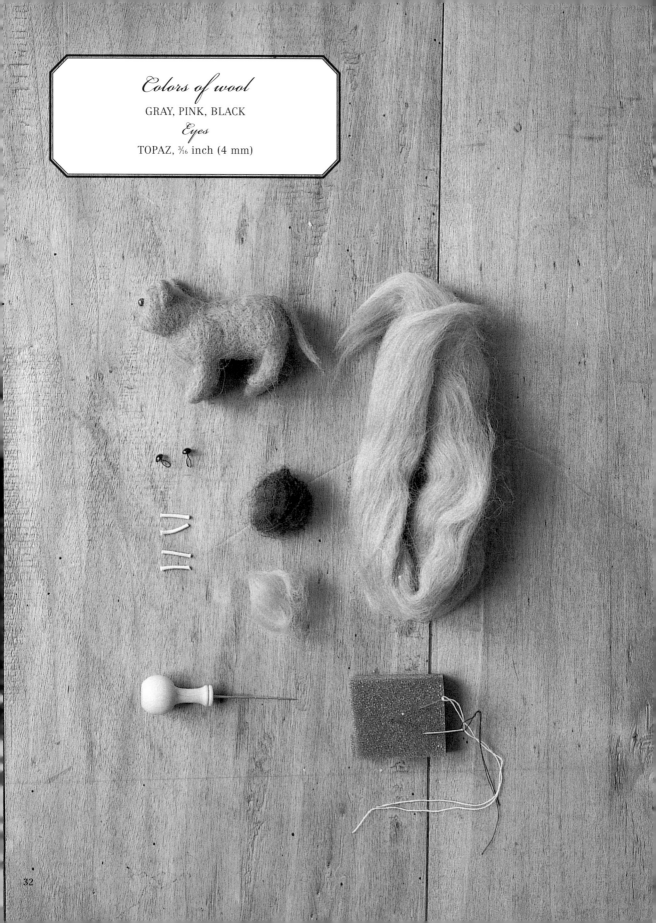

Colors of wool
GRAY, PINK, BLACK
Eyes
TOPAZ, ³⁄₁₆ inch (4 mm)

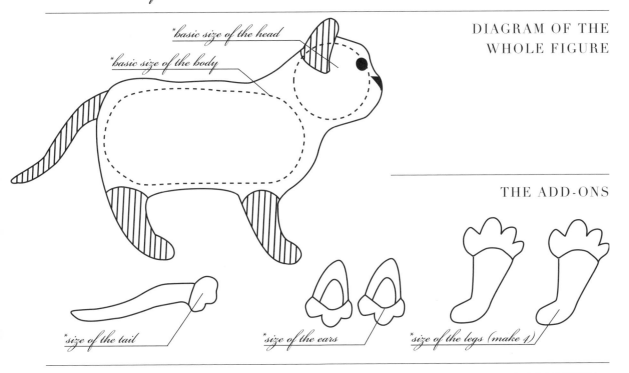

basic size of the head

basic size of the body

DIAGRAM OF THE
WHOLE FIGURE

THE ADD-ONS

size of the tail

size of the ears

size of the legs (make 4)

SHAPING THE BODY

1 Using gray wool, form the basic head and body. Leave an end of unworked wool at the top of the body and join the head and body together by felting the end onto the head with the felting needle.

2 Form the legs using gray wool and short lengths of piping cord (see page 6). Leave an unworked end on each for attaching to the body. Fix them in place by needling these ends to the body.

3 Form two ears from gray wool, needling them to give them the required shape. Leave an unworked end for attaching them to the head. Add a little pink wool to the inner part of each and fix them in place by needling the ends to the head.

4 Using gray wool, form the tail, giving it a slightly curved shape (see diagram). Leave an unworked end and attach the tail by needling the end onto the body.

Finishing touches

Improve the proportions of the body by adding more wool, checking against the diagram for accuracy. Needle sufficient extra wool onto the chest to give it a rounded appearance and onto the front of the head to form the muzzle. Add more around the neck to cover the joint between the head and the neck.

*

Add wool to the legs to enlarge them to the correct size and define the muscles and feet by jabbing with the felting needle.

*

Make a little ball of black wool for the nose and attach to the muzzle with the felting needle. Form the mouth with a fine strip of black wool and use the felting needle to define the lips.

*

Sew on the eyes
(see diagrams on page 6).

7 Welsh Corgi

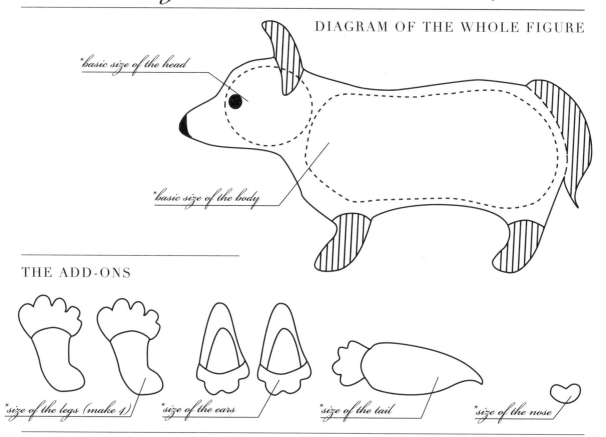

DIAGRAM OF THE WHOLE FIGURE

*basic size of the head

*basic size of the body

THE ADD-ONS

*size of the legs (make 4)

*size of the ears

*size of the tail

*size of the nose

SHAPING THE BODY

1 Form the basic head and body shapes from white wool, leaving an end of unworked wool at the top of the body. Join them together by felting this end onto the head.

2 Form the legs from white wool and strips of piping cord (see page 6). Leave an unworked end on each for attaching to the body. Fix them in place.

3 Form the ears from beige wool, shaping them with the felting needle and leaving unworked ends for attaching to the head. Add a touch of pink wool to the inner parts of the ears and fix them in place.

4 For the tail, take a strip of beige wool and model the pointed end of it with the felting needle. Roll it between your palms to give it its shape and then attach it to the body.

Finishing touches

Add bulk to the head, neck, and chest with extra wool, checking against the diagram for accuracy.

*

Add a layer of beige wool to the upper body, leaving the muzzle, chest, legs, and the underside of the body white.

*

Make the legs more substantial by adding beige wool along the backs. Mark out the muscles clearly, using the felting needle.

*

Needle a little ball of black wool to the muzzle for the nose.

*

Sew on the eyes (see diagrams on page 6).

Colors of wool
WHITE, BEIGE, BLACK, PINK
Eyes
BROWN, ⅕ inch (5 mm)

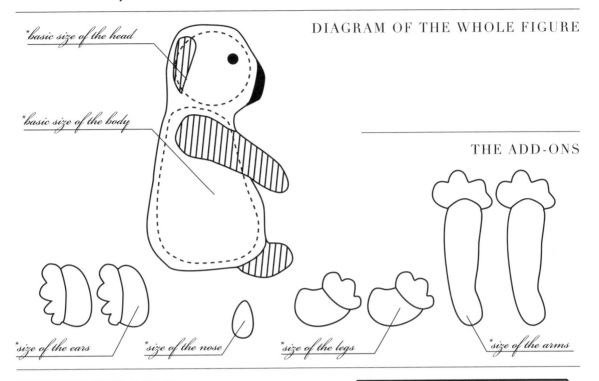

DIAGRAM OF THE WHOLE FIGURE

*basic size of the head

*basic size of the body

THE ADD-ONS

*size of the ears   *size of the nose   *size of the legs   *size of the arms

SHAPING THE BODY

1 Form the basic shapes of the head and body in gray wool, leaving an end of unworked wool at the top of the body. Join the pieces together by felting this end onto the head with the felting needle.

2 Form two arms and two legs from gray wool, reinforcing them with strips of piping cord (see page 6), jabbing them with the felting needle to give them the required shape. Leave an unworked end on each for attaching to the body and fix the arms and legs in place with the felting needle.

3 With the same color, form two ears, needling them into shape. Leave an unworked end on each for attaching to the head. Fix in place by needling these ends to the head.

Finishing touches

Add more wool to improve the body proportions, checking with the diagram for accuracy. Needle extra wool onto the chest to give it a rounded appearance and add more to the neck to cover the joint between the head and the neck.

*

Give more bulk to the legs and arms by adding more wool. Use the felting needle to define the muscles clearly.

*

Needle a layer of white wool onto the stomach.

*

Form the nose out of black wool and fix it to the muzzle with the felting needle.

*

Sew on the eyes (see diagrams on page 6).

Suggestion

Make another, smaller koala.

Turkish Van Cat FELINE FRIEND NATIVE TO TURKEY

RED-BREASTED FRIEND *Robin*

11

Brown Bear HONEY SEEKER

Fox RED AND WILY

Colors of wool
WHITE, BEIGE, PINK
Eyes
GREEN, ³⁄₁₆ inch (4 mm)

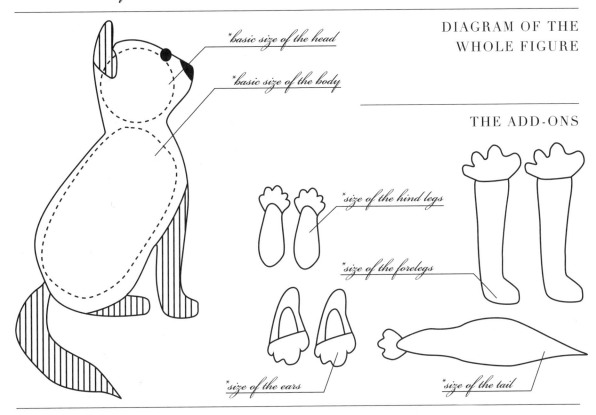

DIAGRAM OF THE
WHOLE FIGURE

*basic size of the head

*basic size of the body

THE ADD-ONS

*size of the hind legs

*size of the forelegs

*size of the ears

*size of the tail

SHAPING THE BODY

1 Using white wool, form the basic head and body, leaving an end of unworked wool at the top of the body. Join the pieces together by felting this end onto the head with the felting needle.

2 Make the forelegs and the hind legs from white wool, reinforcing them with strips of piping cord (see page 6), by rolling the wool between the palms of the hands. Leave ends for attaching to the body. Fix the legs in place with the felting needle.

3 Form two ears, needling them into shape. Add a touch of pink wool to the inner part of each and fix the ears to the head.

4 For the tail, take a strip of white wool and roll it between the palms. Shape it with the needle and then roll it again until it is compact, leaving an end for attaching to the body. Fix the tail in place.

Finishing touches

Improve the body proportions by adding more wool, checking against the diagram for accuracy. Needle extra wool onto the chest to give it a rounded appearance and onto the front of the head to form a muzzle at the neck level.

*

Add bulk to the legs with more wool. Define the muscles by jabbing vigorously with the felting needle.

*

Needle pieces of beige wool over the white wool to form patches on the body and also around the ears.

*

Add a little ball of pink wool to the muzzle to represent the nose.

*

Sew on the eyes
(see diagrams on page 6).

Colors of wool

GRAY, BROWN, ORANGE, BLACK,
MOTTLED LIGHT BROWN

Eyes

BLACK, ³⁄₁₆ inch (4 mm)

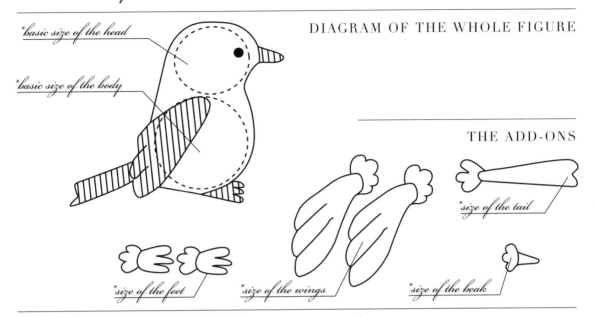

DIAGRAM OF THE WHOLE FIGURE

basic size of the head

basic size of the body

THE ADD-ONS

size of the tail

size of the feet   *size of the wings*   *size of the beak*

SHAPING THE BODY

1 Using gray wool, make the basic head and body, leaving an end of unworked wool on the body. Join the pieces together by felting this end onto the head with the felting needle.

2 Form the tail out of brown wool, jabbing with the felting needle to give it the required shape. Leave an unworked end for attaching to the body. Fix in place by needling the end onto the body.

3 Form the beak from black wool, leaving an unworked end at its base. Fix in place by needling the end onto the head.

4 Form the feet using the mottled light brown wool and giving them the required shape with the felting needle. Leave an unworked end on each for attaching to the body. Fix in place by needling these ends onto the body.

5 Form two wings from brown wool, needling them into the required shape. Leave an unworked end for attaching to the body. Embed some fine strips of gray wool to represent feathers and fix the wings in place by needling the ends onto the body.

Finishing touches

Improve the proportions of the body by adding more wool and checking against the diagram for accuracy. Add some orange wool at the base of the beak. Needle sufficient orange wool onto the chest to give it a rounded appearance and add more brown wool around the back and sides of the neck to cover the joint between the head and the neck.

*

Cover the upper part of the head and back, right down to the tail, with a layer of brown wool.

*

Sew on the eyes (see diagrams on page 6).

Colors of wool
BROWN, BEIGE, BLACK, PINK
Eyes
BLACK, ⅛ inch (3 mm)

DIAGRAM OF THE WHOLE FIGURE

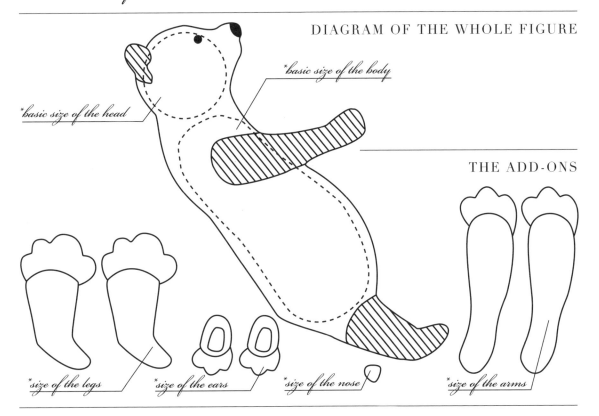

*basic size of the body

*basic size of the head

THE ADD-ONS

*size of the legs　　*size of the ears　　*size of the nose　　*size of the arms

SHAPING THE BODY

1 Using brown wool, form the basic head and body, leaving an end of unworked wool at one end of the body. Join the pieces together by attaching the end onto the head using the felting needle.

2 Form two arms and two legs from brown wool, reinforcing them with strips of piping cord (see page 6). Leave unworked ends for attaching to the body. Fix the arms and legs in place by needling the ends onto the body.

3 Form two ears from brown wool, jabbing with the felting needle to give them the required shape. Leave unworked ends for attaching to the head. Add a touch of pink wool to the inner parts of each and fix them in place by needling the ends onto the head.

Finishing touches

Improve the body proportions by adding more wool, checking against the diagram for accuracy. Needle extra wool onto the chest and stomach to give them a rounded appearance and onto the front of the head to create a muzzle. Add more around the neck to cover the joint between the head and the body.

*

Add bulk to the arms and legs with more brown wool. Define the muscles by jabbing with the felting needle.

*

Add a thin layer of beige around the muzzle, and with the felting needle attach a small ball of black wool to the muzzle for a nose.

*

Sew on the eyes (see diagrams on page 6).

Colors of wool
RUST RED, WHITE, BLACK, BROWN
Eyes
BROWN, ³⁄₁₆ inch (5 mm)

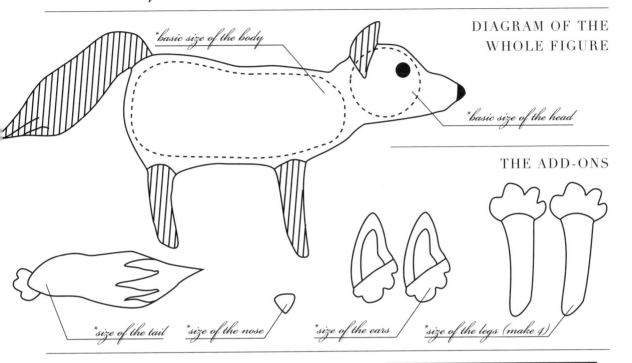

DIAGRAM OF THE
WHOLE FIGURE

*basic size of the body

*basic size of the head

THE ADD-ONS

*size of the tail   *size of the nose   *size of the ears   *size of the legs (make 4)

SHAPING THE BODY

1 Using the rust red wool, form the basic head and body shapes, leaving an end of unworked wool at the top of the body. Join the two pieces together by attaching the end onto the head with the felting needle.

2 Form the legs from rust red wool, reinforced by strips of piping cord (see page 6). Leave unworked ends for attaching to the body. Add a thin layer of brown wool around the ends of each to represent the feet and then fix the legs into place on the body.

3 Form the ears out of the rust red wool, needling them into the required shape. Leave an unworked end for attaching to the head. Add a touch of white wool to the inner parts of the ears and fix them in place.

4 Form the tail with a strip of white wool and jab with the felting needle from the base to the tip, leaving an unworked end at the base for attaching to the body. Cover it with rust red wool, leaving just the tip white. Needle it all over, then mold it by rolling between the fingers. Fix it in place.

Finishing touches

Improve the proportions of the body by adding more wool, checking against the diagram for accuracy. Needle sufficient extra wool onto the chest to give it a rounded appearance and onto the front of the head to create a muzzle. Also add some around the neck to cover the joint of the head to the neck.

*

Add a thin layer of white wool to the chest, stomach, and muzzle, jabbing with the felting needle to fix it.

*

Add more wool to give bulk to the legs. Use the felting needle to define the muscles clearly.

*

Needle a little ball of black wool to the end of the muzzle for a nose.

*

Sew on the eyes
(see diagrams on page 6).

Mice TWO ARE TWICE AS NICE

Dalmatian BLACK-AND-WHITE DELIGHT

SIT UP AND BEG *Jack Russell Terrier*

DIAGRAM OF THE WHOLE FIGURE

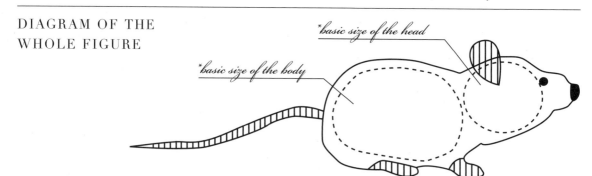

*basic size of the head

*basic size of the body

THE ADD-ONS

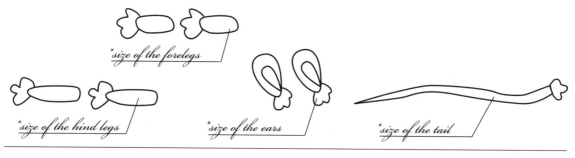

*size of the forelegs

*size of the hind legs

*size of the ears

*size of the tail

SHAPING THE BODY

1 Form the basic head and body from gray wool, leaving an end of unworked wool at the top of the body to attach the head. Join the pieces together by attaching the end onto the head with the felting needle.

2 Form the legs from gray wool, jabbing repeatedly with the felting needle until they are dense and compact. Leave unworked ends for attaching them to the body. Fix the legs in place.

3 Form the ears from gray wool, giving them the required shape with the felting needle. Leave unworked ends for attaching them to the head. Add a touch of pink wool to the inner parts of each and fix them in place.

4 For the tail, take a very thin strip of gray wool and roll it between your palms. Leave an unworked end for attaching to the body. Jab the tail lightly with the felting needle and then roll again between the palms to make it compact. Fix it in place.

Finishing touches

Improve the body proportions by adding more wool, checking against the diagram for accuracy. Needle extra wool onto the chest to give it a rounded appearance. Add wool to the front of the head to form a muzzle and around the neck to hide the joint between the head and the body.

*

Add more wool to give bulk to the legs, using the felting needle to mark out the muscles. Add a few strands of pink wool to the feet for contrast.

*

Needle a little ball of pink wool to the tip of the muzzle for the nose.

*

Sew on the eyes
(see diagrams on page 6).

*

Suggestion

Make another mouse in white wool with pink feet.

Colors of wool
GRAY, PINK
Eyes
BROWN, ⅛ inch (3 mm)

DIAGRAM OF
THE WHOLE
FIGURE

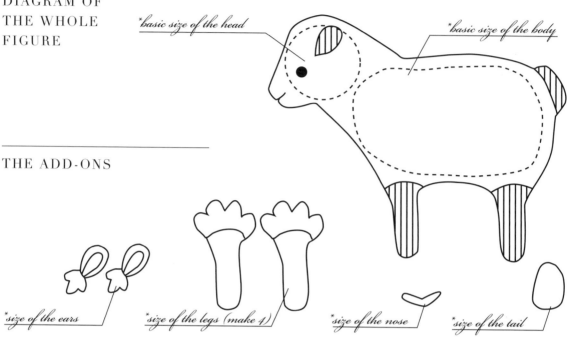

basic size of the head

basic size of the body

THE ADD-ONS

size of the ears

size of the legs (make 4)

size of the nose

size of the tail

SHAPING THE BODY

1 Use mottled gray wool to form the head and use white wool to form the body, leaving an end of unworked wool at the top of the body. Join the pieces together by attaching this end to the head with the felting needle.

2 Form the legs from white wool reinforced with piping cord (see page 6). Leave unworked ends for attaching to the body. Add a thin layer of mottled gray wool to the lower parts of each for the feet and then fix the legs in place.

3 Form two ears from mottled gray wool, giving them the required shape by jabbing with the felting needle. Leave an unworked end for attaching to the head. Add a touch of black wool to the inner parts of each and fix them in place.

4 Form the tail from mottled gray wool (see diagram for shape). Leave an unworked end for attaching to the body. Fix the tail in place.

Finishing touches

Improve the proportions of the body by adding more wool, checking against the diagram for accuracy. Needle sufficient extra wool onto the chest to give it a rounded appearance and onto the front of the head to create a muzzle. Add more around the neck to cover the joint of the head to the neck.

*

Give bulk to the legs by adding more wool. Define the muscles using the felting needle.

*

Needle a thin layer of mottled gray wool to the middle of the back.

*

Needle a thin strip of black wool to the muzzle for the nose.

*

Sew on the eyes
(see diagrams on page 6).

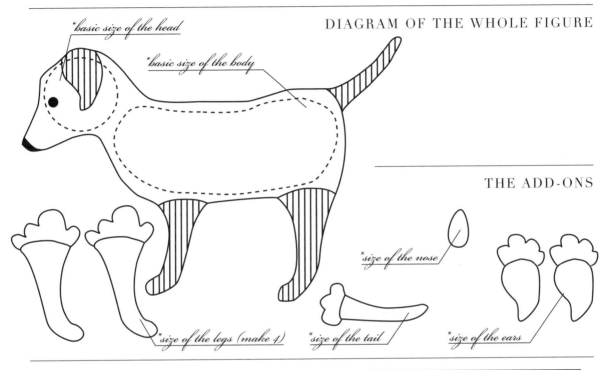

*basic size of the head

*basic size of the body

DIAGRAM OF THE WHOLE FIGURE

THE ADD-ONS

*size of the nose

*size of the legs (make 4)

*size of the tail

*size of the ears

SHAPING THE BODY

1 Form the basic head and body shapes from white wool, leaving an end of unworked wool at the top of the body. Join the pieces together by attaching the end onto the head with the felting needle.

2 Form the legs from white wool reinforced with strips of piping cord (see page 6). Leave an unworked end on each. Fix the legs in place by needling the ends onto the body.

3 Form the two ears from black wool, giving them the required shape with the felting needle. Leave unworked ends for attaching to the head. Fix the ears in place.

4 To form the tail, take a strip of white wool and roll it between your palms. Leave an unworked end for attaching to the body. Needle it until it is compact, then fix it in place.

Finishing touches

Improve the proportions of the body by adding more wool, checking against the diagram for accuracy. Needle sufficient extra wool onto the chest to give it a rounded appearance and onto the front of the head to create a muzzle.
Add more around the neck to cover the joint of the head to the neck.

*

Give more bulk to the legs by adding more white wool. Define the muscles by jabbing with the felting needle.

*

Create the spots on the body by making the round shapes in varied sizes from black wool and then needling them to the body.

*

Make a little ball of black wool for the nose and fix it to the muzzle with the felting needle.

*

Sew on the eyes
(see diagrams on page 6).

DIAGRAM OF THE WHOLE FIGURE

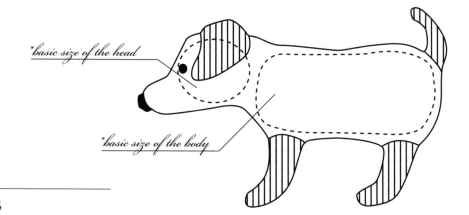

*basic size of the head

*basic size of the body

THE ADD-ONS

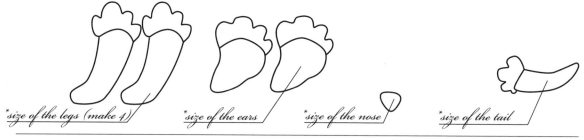

*size of the legs (make 4)   *size of the ears   *size of the nose   *size of the tail

SHAPING THE BODY

1 Form the basic head and body shapes from white wool, leaving an end of unworked wool at the top of the body. Join the two pieces together by attaching the end onto the head with the felting needle.

2 Form the legs from white wool reinforced with strips of piping cord (see page 6). Leave an unworked end on each. Fix the legs in place by needling the ends to the body.

3 Form the two ears from brown wool, needling them into the required shape. Leave unworked ends for attaching to the head. Fix the ears in place.

4 Form the tail from white wool. Leave an unworked end for attaching to the body. Fix it in place.

Finishing touches

Improve the proportions of the body by adding more wool, checking against the diagram for accuracy. Needle sufficient extra wool onto the chest to give it a rounded appearance and onto the front of the head to create a muzzle. Add more around the neck to cover the joint of the head to the neck.

*

Give bulk to the legs by adding more wool. Define the muscles by jabbing vigorously with the felting needle.

*

Add some brown and rust-red patches around the eyes and on the body by forming small quantities of wool into the shapes required and then needling them into place. Make a little ball of black wool for the nose and fix it to the muzzle using the felting needle.

*

Sew on the eyes (see diagrams on page 6).

Colors of wool

WHITE, BROWN, RUST RED, BLACK

Eyes

BLACK, ⅛ inch (3 mm)

Colors of Wool

WHITE, MOTTLED LIGHT BROWN, BLACK

Eyes

BLACK, ⅛ inch (3 mm)

16 *Jack Russell Terrier* (*sitting up*) *Tools required*

DIAGRAM OF THE WHOLE FIGURE

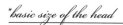
basic size of the head

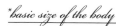
basic size of the body

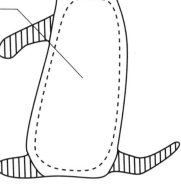

THE ADD-ONS

size of the ears

size of the forelegs

size of the tail

size of the nose

size of the hind legs

SHAPING THE BODY

1 Form the basic head and body shapes from white wool, leaving an end of unworked wool at the top of the body. Make the bottom somewhat flat so the dog will sit up straight. Join the pieces together by attaching the end onto the head with the felting needle.

2 Form the two forelegs and two hind legs from white wool reinforced with strips of piping cord (see page 6), jabbing them repeatedly with the felting needle to give them the required shape. Leave an unworked end on each. Fix the legs in place.

3 Form the two ears from mottled light brown wool, leaving an unworked end on each for attaching to the head. Fix the ears in place.

4 Form the tail in white wool, needling it and rolling it between the palms to make it compact. Leave an end for attaching to the body. Fix the tail in place.

Finishing touches

Improve the proportions of the body by adding more wool, checking against the diagram for accuracy. Needle extra wool onto the chest to give it a rounded appearance and onto the front of the head to create a muzzle. Add more around the neck to cover the joint between the head and the body.

*

Give bulk to the legs by adding more wool. Define the muscles by jabbing with the felting needle.

*

Needle some mottled light brown wool to form the patches around the eyes. Take a little wool and add to the body, needling it to form the required shape.

*

Needle a little ball of black wool to the muzzle to make the nose.

*

Sew on the eyes (see diagrams on page 6).

Good-bye!

Resources

*

YARN AND NEEDLE ART
MANUFACTURERS & DISTRIBUTORS

*

BARTLETTYARNS, INC.
www.bartlettyarns.com
(207) 683-2251

*

CHECKER DISTRIBUTORS
www.checkerdist.com
(800) 537-1060

*

CLOVER NEEDLECRAFT, INC.
www.clover-usa.com
(562) 282-0200

*

FIBER TRENDS, INC.
www.fibertrends.com
(509) 884-8631

*

WISTYRIA EDITIONS
www.wistyria.com
(616) 847-6733

Acknowledgments

*

Thanks to Carl for EVERYTHING!
To Mamà and Papà, to the dolly birds of
"La basse cour," to Rosemarie, Richard,
and Stéphanie. Thank you to Patricia G.
for her secret codes!

First published in the United States in 2008 by
Watson-Guptill Publications, an imprint of
the Crown Publishing Group, a division of
Random House, Inc.,
New York
www.crownpublishing.com
www.watsonguptill.com

Library of Congress Control Number:
2007943307

ISBN-10: 0-8230-1504-1
ISBN-13: 978-0-8230-1504-7

First published in France by Marabout
(Hachette Livre) in 2007
© Marabout 2007

Printed in China

First printing, 2008
Eighth printing, 2014
9